Love Like This

CHRISTINE SILVA-CRUZ

Presentation by *BookLeaf Publishing*

Web: www.bookleafpub.com

E-mail: info@bookleafpub.com

ISBN: 9789357614177

First edition 2023

This is dedicated to:

My parents, Ting & America, whose love taught me how to love others.

My siblings, Amy & Jude, who taught me about tough love when I needed it and who will most likely still be in shock for years to come that I actually got published.

Jon, whose love truly changed who I am and my life forever.

My nieces & nephew, Normandie, Elinor, Arden, Isla & Henry, whose love inspired me to go after my dreams!

I love you all so very much!

Miracle

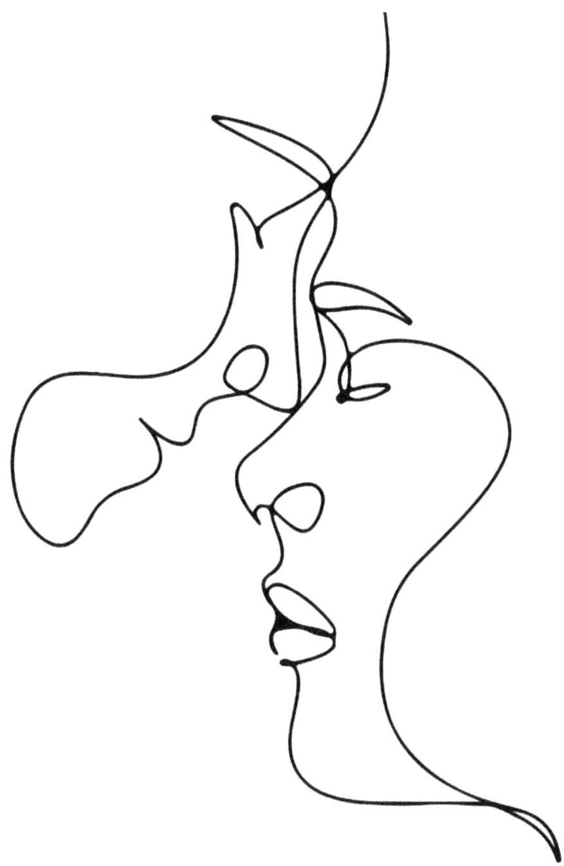

She was Fire
He was Water
But GOD made them fall in love to prove to the
World
That nothing was impossible

How it started

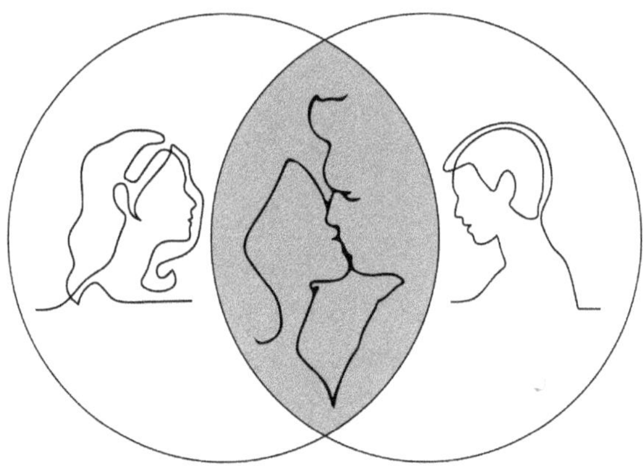

Because he was never shown affection
He fell hard when they kissed
Because she was never heard
She fell hard when he listened
Years later, when she told him what she needed
He had already stopped listening
And that was when she knew
The end of their love story began

Promises

Give me dancing under the stars
Give me flowers just because
Give me affection when I look like a mess
Give me corny jokes because they make me
giggle
Give me sweet notes in random places
Give me anything and everything
But your empty words

Red, Black and White

My favorite colors
He wore them twice
Was that really for me?
My head told me I was crazy
But my heart told me he felt the same
Or maybe the instrument he was truly adept at
playing
Was of someone who loved to break fragile
hearts

Dream

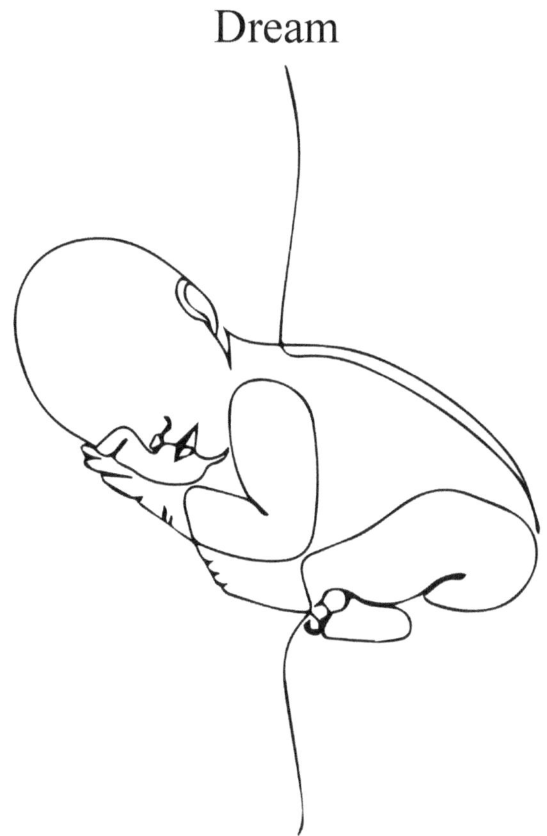

I see you holding the most beautiful baby I have
ever seen
I know this child is yours
I know this child is mine
I know this child is ours
If we are not meant to be
Why does this dream keep haunting me?

Denial

I know you feel the same
Without a word
Your eyes tell me your heart
Your soul already spilled your secrets
Why do you act like you don't care?
Why do you pretend that you do not love me?

Red String

The World did their best
Distance did too
But we were One Soul
Only the Universe really knew
Even Lifetimes could not keep us apart
We were always led back to each other
Two Bodies
One Heart

Before

Before we met
Before our first words
Before our first kiss
Before our first night
My soul was yearning
My heart was longing
For You
It was always You

The Search

In cities full of strangers
In airports full of travelers
My eyes always search for yours
Hoping one day
I will finally be HOME

Long Distance

I write love letters
To you through the Moon
Hoping that I will get your replies
In the morning
From the rising Sun

The Fix

I was so broken
But the magic you made out of silence
On those black and white keys
Put the missing pieces of my heart
Back together
And made me feel like a new
Masterpiece

Fear of Falling

I am scared
He replied "I am too"
But that first kiss was worth
Whatever ending
Awaited them

One Day

Someone will love you so passionately
They will make you forget your heart was ever
broken

Someone will look at the ugliest parts of you
Tell you they are beautiful, making you believe
it too

Someone will see that you are lost in this big,
crazy world
And tell you "You are finally found!"

-Don't you ever give up on LOVE

Love at First Sight

He was easy on the eyes
She told herself "Oh no. Stay away"
But her heart already whispered back to her
"He's the One"

Twin Flame

I lived a life most envied
A happy home
A love so true
But then GOD revealed to me my missing piece
And after that
All my Soul cared about
All my Heart wanted was
YOU

Touch

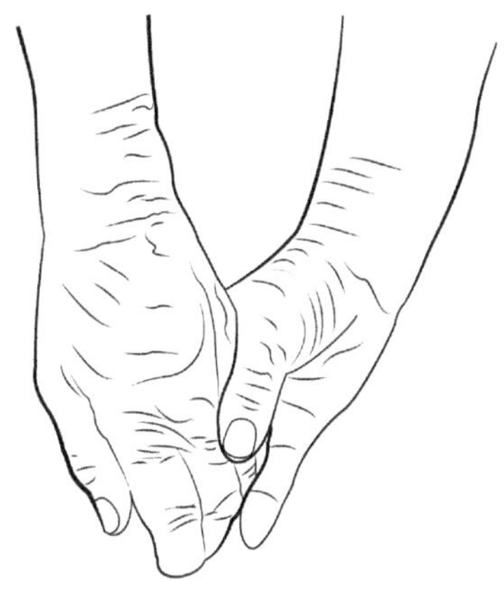

When he held her hand
It dawned on him
That Magic, in fact, was very real
And just like a magician, finding the perfect act
He was never ever letting her go

Drowning

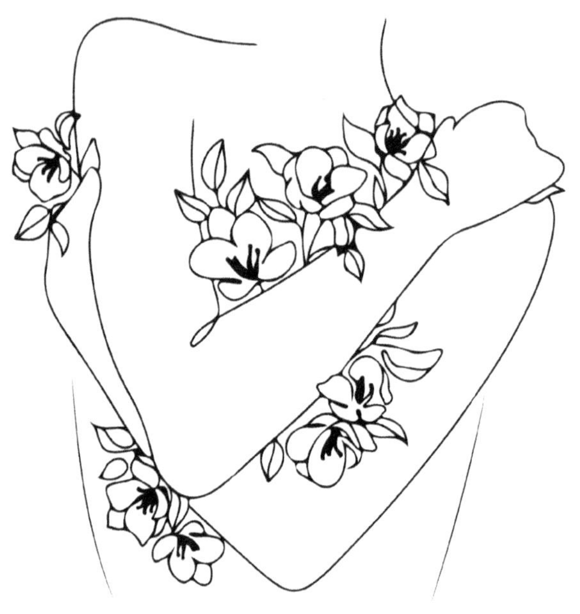

I was not a good swimmer
I always just treaded the waters of this life
But I dove straight into the ocean
of his moonlit eyes
And did not care if I ever took another breath

Passion

Her eyes
Her smile
Her honesty
Her love
She was everything he ever wanted
He manifested and prayed
But when she actually appeared
His broken heart from past hurts rejected her
He could not risk the hurt
Even though he was already hurting, not having
her in his life

Regret

"I hope one day you find someone who loves
you truly"
He pretended he did not read the words
He did not reply
But those words haunted him every day
thereafter
He let go of the one thing that was real
In a world full of fakes

Honesty

I know you love me but are you In love with
me?
He did not need to answer
Because they both knew
And that was all it took
That was the end
No huge fight
Just a simple truth

Angel

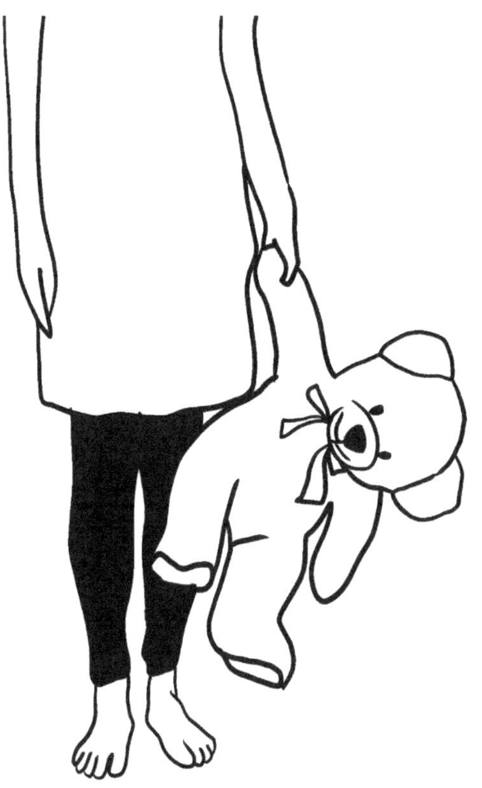

We knew your name before we knew you were
real
We never heard music as beautiful as when we
heard your first heartbeat
We tried hard to keep HOPE away
But she lied to us and told us you would stay
We celebrated and even bought some things
Eight weeks later, she was gone
Along with you and our dreams
Only our broken hearts
And our tears remain